Other books by Author

... more will be revealed soon...

WAR WITHIN

WW V:
Alone, I Roam

Volume 5 of 7

MICHAEL R. BANE

WestBow
PRESS®
A DIVISION OF THOMAS NELSON
& ZONDERVAN

WestBow Press books may be ordered through booksellers or by contacting:

WestBow Press
A Division of Thomas Nelson & Zondervan
1663 Liberty Drive
Bloomington, IN 47403
www.westbowpress.com
844-714-3454

Scripture taken from the King James Version of the Bible.

ISBN: 978-1-6642-3684-4 (sc)
ISBN: 978-1-6642-3685-1 (e)

Print information available on the last page.

WestBow Press rev. date: 06/22/2021

CONTENTS

Chapter 1   I Roam

Chapter 2   Yesterday, Today, Tomorrow

Chapter 3   My Skin

Chapter 4 Rocks and Stones

Chapter 5 Your Face

Chapter 6 My Cage

Chapter 7 This Ink

DEDICATION

Alone, I Roam

I dedicate this collection to my true life hero, my brother. John Bane Jr. You were there for me in my worst/ most insane days. You accepted me into your house, and family. And for the years previously that I was out roaming. You never forgot me. You showed me how a man acts, and does. You are always about others. And I thank you for being about me. You are a reflection of me, and the best parts of me are of you. And I thank you for that, And I love you.

INTRO

Alone, I Roam

The fine line between aloneness, and loneliness. I have experienced both in my life. Though they are the same, they are quite different. There are times that I'm alone, but so much peace, and contentment. And many, many times I'm lonely in a room full of people. I think it may come down to my spiritual condition. At that moment there are still times I feel lonely, but since I invited God into my life I'm no longer alone. And neither are you. God is here for you and so am I. We can do together what I can never do alone....

CHAPTER 1

I ROAM

Amos 8:12a

And they shall wander, from sea to sea, and from the north even to the east. They shall run to and fro.

KJV

WHEN IT WAS WRITTEN

GONE TOO LONG

I've been gone too long
its time to come home

I'm tired of running
these streets I roam

Where do I stop, nothings my own
my aching muscles, my tired bones

My familys all scattered
my children are grown

Feel like I'm in the twilight zone
The places I've been, the people I've known

Theres nothing thats mine
nothings my own.

I've been gone too long
its time to come home

I'm tired of living this life all alone
with nothing that's mine, nothing to show

All this time I've been gone
When does it stop, where do I belong?

There nothing that's mine
nothings my own.

I've been gone too long
its time to come home

RUNNING

How long have I been running?
I lost track of time
days turned to years, and
I think I've lost my mind

How long have I been running?
down these lonely streets I roam
I ran away from everyone
I'm running all alone

When do I stop running?
living this fantasy
To realize life's not what it seems
to face reality

when do I stop running?
to be silent, to be still
to accept my ways not working
to do my fathers will.

So now I must stop running
stop chasing what's not real
to live a life worth living
give myself a chance to heal

So now I must stop running
to open my eyes, to see
to realize, I'm not alone
my God, He lives in me

I REMEMBER

I remember walking for miles
with fire walls on both sides of me,
and I thought my lungs would collapse.
I remember long purposeless days, and
cold empty nights with no love.
I remember eating garbage
not fit for a dog, and never being filled
I was empty
my soul was dead, but yet I lived.
I remember at times I wished for death
and it would not come
it was not my time.
I remember times past, and ages gone
and everything was the same
day after day, nothing would change
darkness grew, and
the light was too bright for my eyes, and
I remember no one there, but me.

Then, I remember
Something within me awoke
I lay on my back, and looked
up at the star filled sky.
I was so small, there alone.
But, I was not alone, God was there
I felt as though I breathed fresh air,
for the first time.
I was quenched, and filled
and hope grew.
then there was love, self love,
With love all things are possible
even change.
change that I thought would never come, came
I stopped living alone.
life had purpose, I had purpose
I remember that day.
I can not forget that day
Unless, I wish to return.

RIVER OF TEARS

I am so close to the river
that can take me away from here.
you saved me from myself
I was drowning.
I was drowning in a river of tears.
From all the pain, from all the years
I was drowning
the loneliness was killing me
I was alone, and lonely
no one was near
And I was drowning
drowning in a river of tears.
I am so close to the river
that can take me away from here
But you saved me from myself
I was drowning
I was drowning in a river of tears.

HIDE AND SEEK

Don't even try it
you can't run from you
you have to face you
there's no other way.
you can't hide from you
playing hide and seek
living alone
with only you.
Running from you
but you are always there.
you can't run far enough
you can't run fast enough
you can't get away from you
you must face you.
Hide and seek won't work
hiding from yourself
you can't hide from you.
Don't even try it
it won't work
you must face you
there's no other way.

CHAPTER 2

YESTERDAY, TODAY, TOMORROW

Matthew 6:34a

Take therefore no thought for the morrow;
For the morrow shall take thought for
the things of itself.

KJV

WHEN IT WAS WRITTEN

TODAY

Thinking about what could have been
    should have been
    would have been
missed opportunities, relationships, love
    all because of a drug
    days, weeks, years lost.
    Freedom, trust, self respect; none
Yesterday gone, it cannot return
tomorrow, is not promised
    all I have is today
    my possibilities are endless
    my goals and dreams are alive
    opportunities, relationships, love
Today, I have hope for a brighter tomorrow
So today, I must forgive myself
today, I will embrace my freedom
today, I will love myself, and others.

STOP LIVING A LIE

One of these days, one of these years
things will change, no more tears
As days go by, I learn to feel
not run away, but accept what is real
So I must hold on just one more day
to learn to laugh, to learn to play
Now it's time to stop living alone
invite you over, or pick up the phone
Now it's time to open my heart
now it's time for a brand new start
one of these days, one of these years
stop living a lie, stop living in fear
to open my heart, and let you in
to open my soul, to love again.
Stop living a lie, there's a better way
to let you in, to start today.

REMEMBER

I remember what you said
that you will love me forever
I remember what you said
that our love will never end
I remember what you said
that you will leave me never
I remember what you said
that I am your best friend
I remember what you said
that my dreams were yours to
I remember what you said
that you will help me through
the good times, the bad times
whatever may come.
I remember what you said
though we're two, we're one

I remember what you said
our love will pass the tests, the trials
I remember what you said
our love can span the miles
though space, and time have us apart
I want you to know
you are still in my heart.
So remember what I said
that I will love you forever
So remember what I said
that I will leave you never
So remember what I said
that you are my best friend.
and that will never end.

NEW LIFE

My new life starts now ...
everyday, a new beginning
more acceptance, and learning
my new life starts now ...
it is a process, not a destination
I must give my all today
without hesitation.
my new life starts now...
filled with decisions
keeping alive my dreams, my visions
my new life starts now ...
I'm purpose driven
yesterday's mistakes, are gone, forgiven
Every day I have what I need
to live victorious, to succeed
my new life starts now...

STOP LIVING ALONE

Have you ever felt helpless, afraid and in doubt,
and sure that things would never work out.
the helpless feelings, alone and in tears,
and pain bottled up over the years.
Not knowing that others felt the same,
all of the guilt, all of the shame.
Its time to realize, there's a better way,
stop living alone, stop running away.
and learn to share, and learn to give,
learn to love, and learn to live.
The time is now, to start today.
Stop living alone, stop running away.
Don't turn back now, you've come too far,
Share what you feel, share who you are.
take your time, take it slow
the time is now, its time to grow,
stop running away, stop living alone.

CHAPTER 3

MY SKIN

Job 19:20

My bone cleaveth to my skin, and to my
flesh, and I am escaped with the skin
of my teeth.

KJV

WHEN IT WAS WRITTEN

PUPPET

The puppet with no strings
    that lives
    it tricks the mind
    it never gives ...
He got me to
    He has a name
    but has no home
From soul to soul
    the puppet roams
    I have nothing now
    that is my own
The puppet with no strings
    his victims left soulless
    it doesn't care, its lawless
    subtle deceit, flawless
Some say wicken lives within
    doesn't realize his life, his sin
Its all he knows
    your soul to win,
    they cut his strings
    yet he still lives ...

BITE THE HAND

Why you fight the man
that needs you?
Will you bite the hand
that feeds you?
you're like an open book
I read you.
You are my favorite wreck
I need you.
But please don't bite
the hand that feeds you.

(18)

Are you demon possessed
or just darkness obsessed???

the distance of 18 inches
from your brain to your heart

and 18 miles from your heart
to your soul

Will the light get brighter
or the darkness grow??

Will you be carried by the light,
or dragged down below??

there's barely a flicker
and the lights getting dim

you must come to your senses
you must run from him

He's licking his fingers
He's counting your sin ...

A WAR ON EVERYTHING

The war within
a war on everything ...

Everything you used to know
everything you used to be.

A war on everything
the war within, misery.

Forget all you used to know
you're not who you used to be.

the war within
A war on everything...

the battle is real
Say good-bye
to all you used to be ...

YOU KNOW ME

You know the things I've said and done
    you know me
    the real me
    all of me
    and yet you help me
you know my deepest secrets
you know my darkest moments
    you know me
    and yet you accept me
    all of me
you know where I've been
    from where I've come
    you know me
    and yet you trust me
you know my hopes, my dreams
    where I want to go
    and yet you hold me
    but not too tightly
    in case I have to go
you know me
    all of me
    and yet you love me

SHINE

Weather I feel it or not
on the outside
It's time to shine
from the inside ...
and though its a
dark, and scary world
on the outside
the river of life
runs on the inside...
the mountain may seem
to high to climb
we are called to
move mountains
Its time to claim
His strength
From the inside ...
So when they look at me
from the the outside
Its Him, they see
from the inside ...

NOT MINE

Cleanse the hate
from deep within
wash the sorrow
from off my skin
Time to clear my path
stop living in the past
I need a reason –
So much pain, I retain
and its not even mine ...
wash the sorrow from
off my skin
that seeps from deep within
so much I retain
that's not even mine ...
I need a reason –

SO CLOSE

So close, but yet so far away
as if I could reach out,
and touch, and smell
the wanting of your breath,
or taste the sweetness of your lips.
So close, but yet;
you are not here
I'm not really sure how
to go on with out you near.
So, I drive myself insane
Why is everything so heavy?
So close, but yet so far
If I could just let go
of the thought of you, and
the sweetness of your lips.

CHAPTER 4

ROCKS AND STONES

Genesis 28:11b

And he took of the stones of that place, and
put them for his pillows, and lay down in
that place to sleep.

KJV

WHEN IT WAS WRITTEN

THAT STONE

Reminded today, by my Lord
when I used that stone
For my pillow
my gratitude, and my comfort
come from that place
He woke me up
every morning at 4:30
And I thanked Him
For that stone, my pillow
Reminded today by my Lord
that He used that same
pillow, that stone
and again I find my
gratitude, and my comfort
and, again I thank my Lord
For that pillow, that stone
and again, its 4:30 am.

THE WALL

I built up a wall, between you and me
built up so high, I could not even see
The wall is so thick, I barely can breathe.
I'm hiding from you, hiding from me.
I look at myself, don't like what I see
And I think I can fix it with a drug, or a drink
The wall surrounds me, I can't even think
And now it's time to tear down the wall
block, by block it crumbles, it falls.
each block represents my defects, my flaws
Before I can walk, I must learn how to crawl
Now I can see, now I can breath
I'm not afraid to let you see me
who I am, what's inside.
This loneliness will finally subside
I never loved, I never tried.
A thousand tears, I know I've cried.
Now it's time to dry my eyes
To tear down the wall, to let you inside.

TIRED

I'm so tired of running from
you and from me.
Been all over this country from sea to sea.
A river bank, a mountain top
I just kept running
I could not stop.
I slowed now and then along the way
But my stop would not be complete
I'm tired of living in total defeat.
So now it's time, it must be time
To show you who I am, what's inside
To let all the pain and fear subside.
Maybe you'll love me if I let you in
this is when my new life begins.

I'm so tired of running, I must stay still
and start climbing up the recovery hill.
leaving behind, the chaotic mess
mending my mind, the psychoticness.
to turn this heart of stone, to flesh.
I'm so tired
tired of being tired.
I must stop, I must stay still
Now I rest, its my fathers will
Now I rest, now I feel
Now I rest, now I'm real
I'm so tired of running
From you, and from me.
Now I rest, my stop; complete.

CUT

As the blood flows through the vein
and the cut releases pain ...
and the cloud becomes rain
then I know the angels cry
and a seed becomes a bloom
and a spark becomes a flame
as if it's just a game
nothing is the same
and everything will change
in a moment, I'm insane
when I cut across the grain
and all my fluids drained
the angels cry, it rains.
and the cut releases pain ...

HERE I AM

Here I am Lord waiting for you
for your love to shine through
Here I am Jesus
Knowing you are near
I am waiting for you
Yes, Lord you are here
My soul is now whole
I am waiting for you
Here I am Father
My spirit and yours are one
and the best is yet to come.
I know you are God, my rock
you alone can save me
Here I am, waiting for you
Knowing you are near
my spirit, and your spirit are one
and the best is yet to come.

GIVE AND TAKE

Take these suspicious eyes of mine
show me truth, show me trust
take these tired feet of mine
let me climb, let me quest
take this thirst of life of mine
give me drink, make me quenched
take these cursed hands of mine
let me give, make them blessed
take this troubled mind of mine
give me peace, give me rest
take this stoney heart of mine
make it new, make it flesh.

FLESH AND BONE

Very well engineered
very well constructed

Very sick, very well
every layer, every cell.

Very well built
not morter, not stone

But skin, and blood
flesh, and bone

every element within
from His hand, the ground

very well built
not mortar, not stone

From the ground
From His hand

Now skin and blood
Now flesh and bone.

CHAPTER 5

YOUR FACE

1 Thessalonians 3:10a

Night and day praying exceedingly
that we may see your face.

KJV

WHEN IT WAS WRITTEN

A STRANGER'S EYES

When you look into a stranger's eyes
tell me what you see ...
Do you see a friend or foe,
or something in between? ...
Do you see hope, or fear,
a nightmare, or a dream? ...
But also you must realize
things aren't always what they seem ...
you never know from where he came
to make it through this far ...
For He could be an angel
who God sent to where you are ...
or maybe there's a purpose
Something you should do ...
Perhaps that person
could be helped by only you...
Don't get me wrong
I'm not saying trust everyone you see...
Some strangers are dangerous
some strangers are mean ...
So I think with all these words I wrote
what I'm really trying to say...
when you look into a stranger's eyes
give that man a break...

JUST FOR TODAY

Now I must stop playing these games
Time after time consequences the same
When will it stop? When will I change?
And live my life just for today
Now it's time to live by faith
What do you think? What do you say?
You tell me there is a better way
you tell me to stick, you tell me to stay
you tell me to feel, and not run away
Why does it seem so hard to obtain?
Its a free gift through His grace
I know that God is in this place.
I hear Him in your voice
I see Him in your face.
But I must stop, I must sustain
and realize together, we have the strength
To make it through just for today.

THE LAND OF THE LIVING

When I choose to live
death loses its grip on me
I turn my back on death
and join the land of the living

And now I see life
my heart lives, and loves
Its because of you
You showed me the way
to the land of the living

And each day I live
and each day I love
Its because of you
But I must choose to live
and stay in the land of the living

I was dead
But now I live
And its because of you
that I am here
In the land of the living

DOPE FIEN MOVE

I saw an old friend
the other day

But when he saw me
He looked away

His skin was yellow
His hair was grey

His lips were burnt
His clothes were stained

He finally asked me
Where I've been

And I told Him
I found a new way to live

I asked Him to come
I told Him its free

I couldn't believe it
When he turned from me

And he said I'm sorry
I have someplace to be

And I thanked God
That way no longer me

FROM WHICH YOU COME

Why does your head
have so many legs?

Moving here and there
I can overlook the colors

But I can't overlook the teeth

Your teeth have eyes
dripping fluids
I know you see all

It frightens me
From which you come

My eyes are closed
I can not escape yours

No I will not go
I must stay here

You must return alone
To there, from which you come

MORE LIKE YOU

I hear what you say
I see what you do
I want to be more like you

I want to learn to laugh and play
To make a difference in someone's day
And be content come what may

I want to be more like you
The things I say
The things I do

To make a difference in someone's day
And be content come what may

CHAPTER 6

MY CAGE

Ecclesiastes 4:14a

For out of prison he cometh to reign.

KJV

WHEN IT WAS WRITTEN

HOW I FEEL

Do you know how I feel?
Can you understand me?
I lived in fear so long
But now I have hope ...
And I want to share with you
How I feel, my hope
I lived in doubt so long
But now I have understanding ...
And I want to share this with you
How I feel, my understanding
Do you know how I feel?
I lived in a cage for so long
But now I have love...
And I want to share it with you
how I feel, my love
I want to share it with you
How I feel ...

WHERE IS MY SOUL?

A heart that's dark
a twisted mind
body not mine
All of this
Where is my soul?
life is over
Now, where do I go?
my spirit lives
too late to change
dust, returns to earth
Where is my soul?
nothing else matters
Now, where will I go?

EMPTY SHELL

I feel like something is wrong with me
Like I am an empty shell
as if someone reached deep inside of me,
and ripped out my soul,
or even worse, something ...

I lived the life I wanted to live
and I paid a terrible price
not many can pay this price
and very few survive,
the symptoms, and consequences
of being an empty shell ...

A head full of angels, and demons
A room full of saints and heathens
trying to take me to heaven, to a cell
and there I sit a lonely, empty shell ...

If I could change the way you see me,
and see that something is wrong
this is not the way I wanted to live,
is it too late for me to change? ...

A room full of saints, and heathens
A head full of angels, and demons
So was this a choice I made?
or a choice made by someone,
or even worse something?...

So am I a victim to this?
or did I truly survive?
Am I dead, or am I alive?
The price is too high
Is this heaven, my cell?
Here I sit a lonely empty shell ...

WAX NIGHTMARE?

Am I awake, or am I asleep?
that space in between
is often so deep –
I struggle to think,
and something takes over
wax nightmares?
unreal, but are
Am I awake, or am I asleep?
visions interrupted
nightmare interlude
almost forced without invite
spiritual rapist, you are
theft of all within
infiltrating yourself
to my very core
Is this fair?
Is this real?
Wax nightmare?
Let go of me, my soul
give me back

I scream, but no one hears
I have no voice
I have no say
I am frightened
I can not get away
I fight to move
you nail me to my bed
you sacrifice me
Am I awake, or am I asleep?
Am I alive, or am I dead?
Wax nightmare?
How do I escape, is it too late?
to free myself from you
or am I your prisoner, always?
My life separate, till death do us part
I sense your danger, I feel no peace
So I know from where you come
I am frightened
I can not get away from you
Wax nightmare

THIS IS FINAL

Standing at the edge of life
laugh at death
that door is closed to no return
darkness encompasses all
so deep, no breath
this is final –
Satan looks and smiles
the last tear falls
pain forever, all hope is gone
this is real
this is final –
no memories, only pain
for the rest of time
too late now
Is this a dream?
Where is the sun?
When will it rain?
Where is God?
too late now
Satan looks and smiles
Darkness encompasses all
All hope is gone
This is final –

MY SECRET

If I told you my secret
Tell me the truth, could you keep it?
Something nobody knows but me
Would you see me differently?
Could it help if I shared?
Would you judge me if I dared?
I close that door, but its still there
Would you listen, would you care?
Its my secret, yes its mine
covered and hidden all this time.
It eats my soul, consumes my mind
It blurs my vision makes me blind
Something nobody knows but me
I must let it go, if I want to be free
So who do I trust, who do I tell?
to escape from my prison this living cell
Its my secret but I understand
Its a part of me, but its not who I am
I must let it go, its what I must do
Its no longer my secret, when I share it with you.

CHAPTER 7
THIS INK

2 Corinthians 3:3b

Written not with ink, but with the spirit of the living God; not in tables of stone, but in fleshly tables of the heart.

KJV

WHEN IT WAS WRITTEN

YOUR WORD, MY SWORD

I pick up my paper
I pick up my pen
it seems its time
to write again...
what will it say?
where will I go?
I have no idea
but, ink I must throw.

So here it is
I open my soul
I am so blessed
He filled the hole ...
You are my God
you're in control
Teach me, reach me
and don't let me go.

We have come so far
there's more, I know
To glorify you
my God, my Lord
which is your word
which is my sword ...

EVERYTHING I NEED

Lonely, but not alone
I just realized I got
everything I need

I just woke up
I'm alone, but not lonely
I got everything I need

Why don't I wanna be here?
cause this is not my home
I'm lonely, but not alone

So as I write
I read between the lines

And I realize
I got everything I need
Except you ...

YOU...

You are my best friend
You make all things possible

You open my eyes.
You close doors, and open others

You speak reality
When no one else does

You are my past, present, and future
You always were
You always will be
You come in so many colors

You show me how to let go
You allow me to let go

You do not judge me
You know my thoughts before I do

You know all of me
You accept me for me

You bring life
You speak love, you speak hate
You bring darkness, you bring light

You know all languages
to you they are one

You are my best friend
You are also my worst enemy

You open my eyes
You bare my soul
You know all

You bring peace, you bring torment.
You ... my pen.

HARD BACK BOOK

What kind of woman
loves like this?

What kind of woman
could love a man like me?

She would have to not only look
but truly see

To read the pages
not just look

Not the cover,
but the book ...

What kind of woman
loves like this?

That could read the story
of a man like me? ...

SO MUCH TO SAY

An old friend
returned for a visit today
He had so much to say
there is not enough time
in just one day.

I introduced him to a
new friend of mine
as they come together
the story unwinds

My old friend, my pen
my new friend, this page
there is so much
that they need to say.

They will never say Good-bye
Forever they will stay
as they come together
my pen, and this page ...

TWO CHAIRS

I see two wooden rocking chairs
Sitting on the porch.
Oh if they could speak
conversations they heard, each.

Ideas, thoughts, and dreams
Shared in that space.
of days to come, and ages past
a couples joys, and pains could last.

Till the day when someone comes along
and makes those chairs their own.
put em on a truck
and took them to their home.

The next phase of their journey
a new spark, new life refreshed.
Sanded smooth, a new stain,
yet the chairs remained the same.

A lot like us, on our journeys
although we change,
parts of us remain ..

And as we continue to grow, to change
to give, and to receive
not much different
than those two chairs, you see
one rocker you, the other me ...

as we share this space, this time
sharing our joys, our pains
our ideas, thoughts, and dreams

though we are two, we are one
in this; the next phase
of our journey ...

YOUR STORY

Everyone has a thought
I'd love to hear your story
of your memories
and of your life
As I write mine on paper
it makes me think of you.
So many thoughts, so many memories
If I could see through your mind's eye
to understand your story
your memories of your life
what makes you who you are
Its what separates you from all,
but also keeps us connected
So many memories, so many thoughts.
As days turn to years
now decades, there gone.
Your story remains
Don't take it with you, it must be told
As only you can tell it.

We share so many memories
But the ones you keep, they are you
Some of them, you may have let go of
those you hold, only you know
if I could see through your minds eye.
to understand your story
what makes you, you
who you are
How you got here.
How you got through
As I write mine on paper
and I think of you
So many thoughts, so many memories
If I could see through your mind's eye
your story remains
do not take it with you, it must be told.

<barcode>III II II III IIIII III IIIIIII III III IIII I IIII III IIIIII III</barcode>

Printed in the United States
by Baker & Taylor Publisher Services